Breaking Free from Addiction

Breaking Free from Addiction

The Journey Back to Father's Design

Pastor Wayne

Xulon Press

Xulon Press
2301 Lucien Way #415
Maitland, FL 32751
407.339.4217
www.xulonpress.com

© 2020 by Pastor Wayne

All rights reserved solely by the author. The author guarantees all contents are original and do not infringe upon the legal rights of any other person or work. No part of this book may be reproduced in any form without the permission of the author. The views expressed in this book are not necessarily those of the publisher.

Unless otherwise indicated, Scripture quotations taken from the New King James Version (NKJV). Copyright © 1982 by Thomas Nelson, Inc. Used by permission. All rights reserved.

Scripture quotations taken from the English Standard Version (ESV). Copyright © 2001 by Crossway, a publishing ministry of Good News Publishers. Used by permission. All rights reserved.

Scripture quotations taken from The Message (MSG). Copyright © 1993, 1994, 1995, 1996, 2000, 2001, 2002. Used by permission of NavPress Publishing Group. Used by permission. All rights reserved.

Printed in the United States of America.

ISBN-13: 978-1-6312-9208-8

Conversations

1. Starting Right Here, Right Now
2. The Wide-Open Trap
3. Breaking Free from the "god" of Addiction
4. Getting to the Root of Addiction: 12 Steps to Freedom
5. Choosing a Mentor to Help Break Your Addiction
6. Healing the Root of Addiction
7. Clean and Sober? Or Just Sober?
8. A Dead Man Did That
9. Nuclear Fallout All Around
10. Reclaiming Lost Trust
11. Re-entering Regular Life
12. Living with Passion and Purpose
13. Telling Your Story

Dedication

This book is dedicated to all the people who have spoken into my life over all these years and encouraged me to do the work of the ministry, according to the call of God that was in me. My greatest cheerleader in the writing of this book has been, of course, my wife Donna, who has always spoken about me far beyond what I could see in myself and believed in me even when I didn't. My Heavenly Father has also sent two men who have come alongside me to encourage me. I think I have the wool pulled over Leon Brown's eyes as he thinks I am one of the smartest people on the planet! And Lenard Richmond, who is now living free from his earthly body, walked with me through some incredible life changes and the early years of street ministry. Butch Hodge was the pastor who taught me the greatest lesson of all—the Father is love, and it's all about love.

Finally, my earthly father, who I am named after, set an example of going out into the slums of Milwaukee to pick up children on a bus to feed them and teach them the way of Christ. That is where the seed of Grace United Urban Ministry was planted in me. This book is dedicated as a tool to help bring people out of addiction and into the way of Christ.

Table of Contents

Conversations. v
Dedication vii

Starting Right Here, Right Now. 1
The Wide-Open Trap 5
Breaking Free from the "god" of Addiction . . 9
Getting to the Root of Addiction:
   12 Steps to Freedom 15
Choosing a Mentor to Help Break
   Your Addiction. 23
Healing the Root of Addiction. 29
Clean and Sober? Or Just Sober? 37
A Dead Man Did That 43
Nuclear Fallout All Around 49
Reclaiming Lost Trust. 55
Re-entering Regular Life 63
Living with Passion and Purpose 69
Telling Your Story 75

Starting Right Here, Right Now

"Taking the Power to Live Whole Again to the Streets"

"The Spirit of the Lord is upon me, because he has anointed me to proclaim good news to the poor. He has sent me to proclaim liberty to the captives and recovering of sight to the blind, to set at liberty those who are oppressed, to proclaim the year of the Lord's favor." Luke 4:18-19 (ESV)

This is a book, but I would rather you read it as a conversation between the two of us. We'll just talk through each chapter like real people, share a little Scripture, and pray together before we move on to the next chapter.

So, let's start by introducing myself. I'm Pastor Wayne from Grace United Urban Ministry.

My wife Donna and I have been working in mission and outreach ministry for most of our married lives. Together, we have seen firsthand how addiction rips through lives like a tornado, destroying everything in its path. We've seen how addiction issues have broken people just like you. Throughout this book, we are going to talk with you about addiction from what we have learned by working with people who are probably very much like you, people who feel powerless to overcome addiction. Our mission is to *take the power to live whole again to the streets.*

Now, I don't know where you are at or what condition you are in as we share this book together, but my prayer is that we reach you in time and that this conversational book is a divine appointment for us to get together and see an amazing transformation in your life.

I wonder where you are at today. What might your battle with addiction be, and what road did you travel to get there? I wonder what path of destruction addiction took on its path to destroy your life. While many people remain functional to some degree in jobs, too many people lose jobs, homes, family, friends, and, more than anything, their own self-respect. I tell people on the streets that everyone has a name and everyone has a story, and we'd like to know your name and listen to your story. My hope is that what I have to share applies to your story.

There are some things about you that I already know. I know chances are we have never met nor talked before. Nevertheless, let me tell you what I know about you. I know that God, your Heavenly Father, loves you and that you and I are absolutely alike. No, I don't have any deep-seated addictions that I know of, other than dark chocolate! But you and I are both made in the image of God, and our life within us is the life He gave us. That means you are a person with incredible value. You don't feel that way? That's okay because I believe you will by the end of this book.

The fact is, we're having this conversation right now because your Heavenly Father is reaching out to you. He is going to deliver you from the brokenness of addiction and reveal Himself in you as the power to live whole again. I want to personally thank you for spending this time with me as we converse through these few chapters. So, let's take a minute to do what we'll do at the end of each chapter, and let's pray.

Heavenly Father, I want to thank you for my friends who have stopped today to share some time with me. Together, we invite You to be in the midst of each conversation we have throughout this book. I thank you that You know exactly where my friends are right now and that You know their entire story. No matter how broken my friends may be, I thank you that You have never left them nor forgotten them. While You have always been speaking to them, I pray that right now You will increase their ability to hear Your voice as we move forward. I believe, Heavenly Father, that my friends will have an experience with You and that they will know Your incredible love for them and the value You placed upon them. Bless this time we have together.

Amen.

I'll meet you in our next conversation, "The Wide-Open Trap."

Pastor Wayne and Donna Heins
Grace United Urban Ministry
GUUM.faith

The Wide-Open Trap

"Watch and pray that you may not enter into temptation. The spirit indeed is willing, but the flesh is weak." Matthew 26:41 (ESV)

Have you ever seen or heard of a Venus fly trap? No, it's not something you buy in the pest control area of the hardware store! It's actually a plant. The leaves are able to snap shut after a few stimulations of the trigger hairs by a beetle or spider. The more the insect struggles, the more the leaf produces the digestive enzymes to dissolve the bug and consume it for food. A Venus fly trap is absolutely fascinating, unless of course you are the bug that got caught!

Describing your recent past may be like telling the story of one of these bugs we've been talking about. You were just innocently going through life and one day, you landed in the wrong spot. After all, we both know that no one wakes up and says, "I'm going to work really hard over the next thirty days to become a hard-core addict and see if I can destroy my life." But the problem is that once you landed in the wrong spot, the more that situation began to work to eat you up and leave you as nothing but a shell of your former self, just like the beetle and the Venus fly trap.

I thought we might look at some of the wide open traps that can snap shut on any of us at any time. It, in these examples, is the addictive substance, and the story that goes with each "it" is the trap. So, here goes a short list of some traps. Do any of them ring a bell?

- I just tried it on a dare...I never thought it would do this to me.
- I just used to get through class or through finals or to deal with the crying baby.
- Everyone else was doing it...I just didn't want to be made fun of.
- There was nothing else to do in this god-forsaken town.
- It's what my family did; I thought everyone did it.

- It felt really good…until it didn't, and then it felt really bad.
- It took the pain away…for a while, and then the pain wouldn't go away.
- It was my friend; it just helped me chill… until I chilled out of regular life.
- I never would have made it without it… until I couldn't make it without it.
- I thought I was tough and could handle it…I thought wrong.
- I thought it helped me cope and manage my life better…until it managed me.

Can you identify or remember the trap that addiction laid for you? It's important to think about this because the addiction issue you have now is just one of many you could fall into. The more aware you are of the traps, the wiser you can be to avoid any more.

If any of you lacks wisdom, let him ask God, who gives generously to all without reproach, and it will be given him. James 1:5 (ESV)

Let's pray. Heavenly Father, I come to You today with my friends. We thank you that in everything that they have had to walk through that You kept them. Today, we are asking You to pour Your wisdom out to them to open their eyes to see the world around them from Your perspective. I pray that they see differently than ever before and that they see the traps of this world that would draw them into the bondage of addiction. Cause my friends to hear Your voice with a greater clarity than ever before. We especially thank you that no matter where we have been or what we have done that You never leave us nor forsake us. Your love, grace, and mercy toward us is without end, and for that, we praise You.

Amen.

I'll meet you in our next conversation, "Breaking Free From the 'god' of Addiction."

Breaking Free from the "god" of Addiction

"I am the LORD, and there is no other, besides me there is no God; I equip you, though you do not know me." Isaiah 45:5 (ESV)

Well, you made it to the third chapter. You reading this is a divine appointment for you if you struggle with addiction. My heart breaks after seeing so many lives ruined battling the false power of addiction out in the streets, shelters, and every level of our culture.

In addiction, you lose your sense of value as soon as you bow down as a slave to your addiction, and you lose your self-worth as you feel powerless to fight it. You become deceptive in trying to hide it, lose your morals when you steal to support it, and end up shameless when you can't hide it and beg for another fix.

Addiction is woven into the fabric of homelessness. Too often, addiction costs you employment, wears your family out until they give up on you, steals the money to keep a roof over your head, and leaves you without a spouse and with your kids in DHS custody.

Listen to me—there is more to life than alcohol and drugs. In truth, alcohol and drugs are simply a slow, suicidal death. Addiction may dull a pain or bring relief for a short period of time, but it steals your money, robs you of health, dulls your senses, and imprisons you in emotional instability and hopelessness long before the actual prison bars swing shut. So, you end up struggling to survive on the street or at least living below the way you used to live, not realizing the vehicle that got you here will never get you back. Let's say it like it is—addiction is a primary reason homeless people get stuck on the street.

Let me say it this way to you. Addiction has become your god. No way, you say? Well, you look to addiction as your healer because it takes away your pain, at least for a while. You look to addiction as your peace – because it helps you forget and just chill. You look to addiction as your joy, at least when you are high. You give an offering to your addiction every time you spend money on it. You give it your potential, your health, and your best relationships. You leave everything and everyone to spend time with your addiction. You didn't set out to end up here, but you did. Your addiction is your god, and you seemingly have no control over it—it leads you and guides each day.

Maybe the most important thing for you to hear today is that the last statement is a lie. Your addiction does not have to control your life. There is a God, let's call Him your Heavenly Father, who has the power to break that addiction. Don't get me wrong, it's not all on Him. There are some things you must help with. First, you need to have faith, which simply means to agree with God that He has the power to break your addiction and that your addiction has no real power except what you give it.

You need to know God. your Heavenly Father, who can break the power of addiction in your life, and you need to come into agreement with God, change your mind about your addiction, and declare that it has no power. You need to declare that you are not a slave to any substance, not a slave to any way of thinking, not a slave to any controlling or manipulative person, not a slave to a poverty mindset, and not a slave to self-pity or hopelessness.

I want to challenge you today to look at yourself differently. See yourself healed, recovered, whole again, and strong. I want to challenge you today to seek out a support network that believes in you and make yourself accountable to godly people who love you and care about you. Be transparent in how you think and where you are at on the road to recovery and restoration. Seek out people who will speak into your life the power, love, and acceptance of God.

The real living God, your Heavenly Father, is waiting to help you break free from your past god of addiction. The god of addiction has tried to spoil and take your life, but your Heavenly Father, as the Spirit of God within you, gives you freedom—freedom to live as He designed you, freedom to live, and freedom to love and be loved.

I have so enjoyed our conversation in this chapter today. I want to take a moment and pray that the power of God, your Heavenly

Father, would break the power of addiction in your life. He is the power to live whole again!

See what kind of love the Father has given to us, that we should be called children of God; and so we are. The reason why the world does not know us is that it did not know him.
1 John 3:1 (ESV)

Let's pray: Heavenly Father, we just want to thank you that no matter where we are today and no matter what condition we are in right now that You unconditionally love us and that You are our Heavenly Father. We come to You transparent, honest, and open. We need Your help. We need a breakthrough. We need the power of God right now to set us free in our minds, in our emotions, and in our physical bodies. We turn from addiction, we reject it as our master, and we declare that it has no power over us. We ask for supernatural peace and for cleansing in our minds, will, and emotions. Purge our body of all the contamination of addiction and restore our health. Lead us to

Christian brothers and sisters who will love us and support us as we begin a new walk and new season of life. Speak to us, Father, and show us Your grace, mercy, and peace. We look for healing and restoration to bring us into the fullness of what You desire for us. Thank you for loving us and forgiving us.

Amen.

I'll meet you in our next conversation, "Getting to the Root of Addiction: 12 Steps to Freedom."

Getting to the Root of Addiction: 12 Steps to Freedom

No temptation has overtaken you that is not common to man. God is faithful, and he will not let you be tempted beyond your ability, but with the temptation he will also provide the way of escape, that you may be able to endure it. 1 Corinthians 10:13 (ESV)

Together, we are going to dig in a little deeper now. Remember, wherever you are at right now, this is a divine appointment for you to break free from the bondage of addiction. Read and re-read these 12 Steps to Freedom, study them, and ask God, your Heavenly Father, to help you walk out these 12 Steps. You can chop the top off your addiction for a few hours or even a few days. But until you get to the root of addiction, it will always come back. Real freedom can be yours. Let's start right now.

- Stop living in denial. Admit you have an addiction problem. Admit you can't stop it any time you want to, or you would already be clean and free.

- Addiction usually is a mask for pain. Pain is usually unhealed trauma—it points to a crisis that you never finished dealing with. So, name the pain and bring the trauma out into the open. Nothing left in the dark or in secret ever changes.

- Admit you don't have the coping skills to deal with the pain or the addiction. Be honest that you haven't been able to heal on your own.

- Lean hard on your God, your Heavenly Father. Look to Him as the only real power and understand that the only power addiction has is the power you give it. Realize that addiction has ruled as the master in your life. You served the master of addiction as its slave only through the power you gave to it.

- Begin to take control of your life again. Declare that cigarettes, beer, wine, weed, crack, prescription pain killers, gambling, pornography, and negative self-defeating mindsets have no power anymore.

- Here is a big one—ask God as your Heavenly Father to break every power of addiction in your life. Thank Him for being with you and in you every minute of every day as you begin to walk free again. Lean in heavy on Him. He never leaves you nor forsakes you.

- Exercise faith (just agree with God). *He made you in His image*. Agree with Him. Jesus said, *you shall know the truth and the truth shall set you free (John 8:32)*. The truth is that *there is only one Lord and there is no other*, so addiction can no longer lord itself over your life.

- Get a mentor, someone who will disciple you in grace, mercy, and the peace of God. Change your environment from people co-dependent with you in addiction to people you can depend on to help you walk free.

- Don't expose yourself to unnecessary temptation. Find a new hangout. Don't go to those spaces that are filled with what you are removing from your life. When it can't be avoided, do something different. Stand up for yourself instead of bowing down. Boldly say no and walk away. *Set your mind on things above (Colossians 3:1)*, on the things God your Heavenly Father has for you, instead of what the dark world has for you.

- Live one day at a time. If necessary, just live one hour or five minutes at a time. Live free in this moment. Don't dwell on the past, and don't worry about the future. Are you free right now? Celebrate right now. Celebrate every little victory.

- It's been a control issue. Addiction has controlled you, and you are breaking free and taking back control of your life—taking control of how you feel, what you think, how you see yourself, and what you crave. You and your Heavenly Father have had a family meeting, and He is running the bully of addiction out of your life.

- God loves you no matter what kind of addict you've been. He's always loved you, even when you didn't love yourself, love others, or even love Him. Addiction has never loved you. It has always wanted to destroy you. Thank God for His love, His power in your life, His wisdom and guidance, and that He is always listening to you and speaking to you. He is your Heavenly Father. Let Him care for you.

Listen, there is no magic in the 12 Steps to Freedom. When you ask God for help, freedom may come instantly, or it may be a journey. If you fall down, get back up one more time. Don't hide, don't deny, don't lie, and don't quit. You lost a lot of relationships and a lot of time and money getting addicted. Spend yourself to get free. Fight to live the life that God planned for you. When you stop bowing down to addiction and admit you hate your current lifestyle and are shamed by who you've become, you can begin to discover the real you is full of *love, joy, peace, patience, kindness, goodness, faithfulness, gentleness and self-control (Galatians 5:22-23).* That describes a you that you can love and a you that can really love others.

Our time in this chapter of conversation today is going to be life-changing for you. I want to take a moment and pray that the power of God, your Heavenly Father, would break the power of addiction in your life. He is the power to live whole again!

> **Let's pray.** Heavenly Father, we thank you that no matter how many times or how hard we've tried to come out of addiction, You have never given up on us. We confess we can't beat addiction on our own. Heal us at the root of our pain and deliver us from every past trauma. Let the grace, mercy, and peace of God work like a salve deep within us. Change our being so we can change our doing. Cleanse our minds to see us as You see us—made in Your image, free from

bondage, living the God kind of life. Give us wisdom to avoid temptations and live a new life as Your sons and daughters. Thank you for loving and forgiving us.

Amen.

I'll meet you in our next conversation, "Choosing a Mentor to Help Break Your Addiction."

P.S. Remember to just camp out each day in these 12 Steps even as you move on through the following chapters. The conversation in this book is not a race to the finish. It is a transformation in progress. You'll be the first one to know when that transformation is finished.

Choosing a Mentor to Help Break Your Addiction

What you have learned and received and heard and seen in me—practice these things, and the God of peace will be with you.
Philippians 4:9 (ESV)

I have a question. Do you realize how much we need each other? We were made to need each other. That's why in Psalms 68:6, the Bible says God sets the solitary in families. Nobody is supposed to be alone. The problem is that when we've entered the darkness that is addiction, we end up pushing the people we really need around us, away from us. What we fail to understand in the middle of the dark storm is that hurting people don't heal in isolation. Nothing changes until it is brought out into the light. That's why we say healed people heal people and hurting people hurt people.

Listen to me right now—today, you are either healing people or hurting people. What you are doing to the people around you reveals what is going on inside of you. People with addictions are constantly hurting themselves, and that means they are hurting others around them. While you may have pushed your natural family away, there are friends and mentors who can stick closer than a natural brother at times.

The first thing I want you to hear today is how important it is for you to find a godly mentor who will love you where you are at and walk you through the process of breaking free from addiction—someone who has the wisdom, knowledge, and compassion to help you re-integrate back into a normal life. There are some things to know when looking for a mentor. For instance, you just can't get advice from someone who is wearing the same shoes of addiction as you. You may think of them as your friend, but they have no real wisdom or advice that you need. Your new mentor could be someone from your past, but chances are you have pushed them all away and it will be very difficult for them to speak the truth to you without thinking they're judging you. My experience is that the best mentors have not known you long enough to have given up on you, but they know how you are in your addiction and still have enough grace and mercy to speak the truth in love. Did you hear that? — speak the truth to you.

The second thing I want to tell you is that your new mentor is not responsible for where you are or how you got here. You can't react and treat him or her like the parent that put you out of their house, the spouse that left you, or the employer who wouldn't pay you to not show up or do poor quality work. Your mentor needs to understand how you got into addiction, but he or she doesn't want to rehearse all your drama and baggage every day. A good mentor has one simple motivation. He or she is simply an accountability partner who invests time in you to see you break free and transform your life. He or she wants to see you let go of the past, forgive yourself, forgive others, get healed, and take charge of your life again. A good mentor wants to see you clean, recovering in your physical body and in your emotions, and dealing with life without chemical stimulants or perverted thoughts or imaginations.

A good mentor is not a doctor you see so he or she can fix you. <u>A good mentor talks with you to help you change the way you see you</u>—to see yourself whole instead of broken, free instead of in bondage, and free to pursue your God-given purpose and the dream He put in you from the beginning.

Maybe the most important thing for you to know today is that your mentor is going to spend more time talking to you about your identity than your behavior. Your behavior always flows out the person you believe yourself to be on the inside. If you believe you have value, you will treat yourself and carry yourself as someone who has value. If you believe you are worthless, you will treat yourself as disposable. That is why a good mentor is less concerned with your addiction than with your identity. He or she wants to talk about the solution instead of always rehashing the problem and wants to leave you with hope and not condemnation. He or she wants to help you set your mind on something higher than the bottomless pit of addiction, which is a description of the hell you are presently living in, and wants to talk to you about living again as the image of God and walking in love as He is love. A good mentor will talk to you about how God your Heavenly Father is waiting to celebrate your return from darkness into the light of the life He has planned for you.

Finally, when you do approach someone about being a mentor to walk through breaking free from addiction, you need to have a heart to heart. You need to know that he or she believes in the power of God to set you free, and you need to know he or she really loves you. <u>You need to give your mentor permission to speak into your life</u> and be honest with you.

I want to pray with you today that you commit to find the mentor that God has for you and that you experience the two-are-better-than-one principle—that you come out of isolation into a real God-given relationship and that you experience healing from the pain of every past trauma so you can walk out of addiction and into freedom.

> **Let's pray.** Heavenly Father, we come to You today thankful that You know us, that You even know us better than we know ourselves. Father, You know where

we are and exactly what we need. We are asking You right now to bring a divine appointment of relationship into our lives. Lead us and guide us to a mentor and lead and guide that mentor to us. Join us together with someone who will have compassion and understanding with us and at the same time lovingly speak the truth into our lives. Join us with someone who will look past all the pain and failure of our past and speak to us about the future that You have always had planned for us. We thank you right now for every individual that You cause to cross our paths with encouragement, and we thank you for the strength to stand up and walk away from every influence that brings us into bondage. Thank you, Father, for our healing in spirit, soul, and body.

Amen.

I'll meet you in our next conversation, "Healing the Root of Addiction."

Healing the Root of Addiction

He answered, "Every plant that my heavenly Father has not planted will be rooted up."
Matthew 15:13 (ESV)

John was soft-spoken and didn't have the dirty and beat down look of someone sleeping outside in back alleyways. He saw us gathered up to pray with about twenty homeless folks that we had given meals and some clean clothes. When we said amen, he was standing outside our circle with tears in his eyes. One of our ministry team members noticed him and went to greet him. John, contrary to the norm, immediately asked for us to pray with him to be delivered from addiction. He had been to different rehabs, and nothing he had tried had worked in the past. I called one of our pastors who had won a serious personal battle with addiction over to pray for John. When Pastor

Josh was finished, I asked John if I could speak further into his life. I told him that addiction almost always has a root in unhealed trauma. Pastor Josh had prayed a powerful prayer, but it was likely that John would have to cooperate with that prayer by identifying the root of his addiction and applying that prayer directly to the root. John suddenly busted out with his story. He and his wife had a son who they lost at a very young age to cancer. The stress of dealing with cancer, the resultant death, and him being so young was more than they could handle. Soon after, John lost his job, lost the house, and he and his wife divorced. This is trauma with a capital T. John took to drinking to numb the pain and deal with the loneliness. Remember the chapter on traps? Alcohol numbed the pain until it didn't. It numbed the pain until the addiction caused pain of its own.

The sad part of this story, besides that it is true, is that if you simply change the names and a few circumstances, it suddenly sounds like your story. John was bold enough and desperate enough to come over to our mobile mission and ask for prayer. Prayer to overcome addiction is great. Wisdom says find the trauma and target the prayer more specifically and you heal the pain at the root. Prayer does bring the power to heal into everyday real life. John's story is powerful concerning our conversation right now. The power to not drink for a while would not be John's long-term answer. Healing the trauma of family loss was the long-term answer to his addiction to alcohol.

Do you remember me telling you that, "You can chop the top off your addiction for a few hours or even a few days, but until you get to the root of addiction, it will always come back"? Right now, we need to focus in on how we keep addiction from raising its ugly head up over and over again in the future. Addiction needs to die and stay dead once and for all. Real freedom can be yours, so let's get to it.

It would be wonderful if the root of addiction was the same for everyone and we could just develop a medical cure. Unfortunately, that is not the case. While most roots of addiction fall into a few different categories, everyone's root of addiction is somewhat unique to them. So, what is your root? It depends on you, your make-up, what you have been through, and the family and local culture you grew up or lived in at the time your addiction began. I want to stop here and say, I don't refer to it as "your addiction" to label you or bind you in those words but to help you understand it is your personal situation that you have to deal with. <u>It's your bondage that you have to break free from, and nobody else can do it for you</u>.

If you grew up in a home filled with addiction, then the partaking and behavior of those particular addictions is subliminally understood to be normal. Maybe it wasn't in your home, but it had overtaken the neighborhood or the school. The local culture puts a pressure on you to fit in to the culture by joining them in addiction. It's a "we do what we do" mentality without any thought for a life better than what they see in front of them every day. The root of your issue might be low self-esteem, where you didn't think you were capable of standing up on your own and saying "No." The need for acceptance pulled you into something you could see you didn't want because you wanted the benefit of being accepted or were too afraid to fight for your rights.

Most often, people fall into addiction because they can't cope with stress or they have experienced a trauma and addiction becomes the pain management system for the unhealed trauma over time. I actually know some alcoholics on the street who were clean and sober when they got there. After a winter on the streets drinking wine at night to help feel warm or taking some form of speed to stay awake and tend a fire in order to not freeze to death, they found themselves an addict after their first winter. Then, some people spent so long a time in pain and stress that it became their norm, and believe it or not, they created or made pain and stress for themselves to feel normal.

I want to leave you with this thought from the Bible. Abram was a man who God made a covenant with to bless him above all people on the earth at that time. The problem was that Abram lived in a heathen country with an idol-worshipping father and family. The blessing of the covenant with Abram was that if he would leave the heathen neighborhood and his idol-worshipping family and go to a land that God would show him, then God as his Heavenly Father would bless him above all others and give him a son and make Abram a new kind of father.

Your breakthrough may come just by identifying the root and asking God to get healing. Then again, your healing may require a new start, not a running away but a new start to a new life where you can heal and become strong. Then you can see what God has to say about your return to heal and bring life to hurting people where you once lived.

> **Let's pray.** Heavenly Father, we thank you that no matter how many times or how hard we've tried to come out of addiction, You have never given up on us. We confess we can't beat addiction on our own. Heal us at the root of our pain; deliver us from every past trauma. Let the grace, mercy, and peace of God work like a salve deep within us. Change our being so we can change our doing. Cleanse our minds to see us as You see us—made in Your image, free from bondage, living the God kind of life. Give us wisdom to avoid temptations and live

a new life as Your sons and daughters. Thank you for loving and forgiving us.

Amen.

I'll meet you in our next conversation, "Clean and Sober? Or Just Sober."

Clean and Sober? Or Just Sober?

And do not get drunk with wine, for that is debauchery, but be filled with the Spirit.
Ephesians 5:18 (ESV)

The strangest thing happened to me the other day. I was visiting with someone about this book, and this person was telling me about a conversation they had with another addict. The other person said she was clean and sober, so now, people should be helping her. The man I was with said, "I told her that as long as she had the taste in her mouth, she might be sober, but she sure wasn't clean yet." The taste in your mouth. That's what hit me in that conversation.

You see, to be sober means to not be under the influence. We think that means, *I haven't tied one on lately, so I'd pass the pee test.* What sober means in real life is, *I haven't had one in while, but you know I'm probably going to real soon.* Sober is sort of like putting an unruly child in timeout. He or she is not throwing things only because there is nothing in his or her hand at the moment and you haven't left the room.

Clean is a word that goes a little deeper. Just because you're sober doesn't mean you are clean. Clean means it's been a long time. It means you have stood against some pretty mean temptations and held your ground sober. But clean goes a step further. To really be clean, you must be clean long enough to cleanse the toxins out of your system, so you don't want to use to stop feeling sick and feel better by using. To be clean is to see it and smell it and not have that taste flood your mouth like you're starving and looking at the last chocolate bar in the vending machine.

I would describe it from my experience like this. I had to be on a gluten-free diet for about three years. If you only knew how I loved good bread! I'm a connoisseur of fine bread and butter or gravy. Now understand, I'm not comparing my bread addiction to your addiction because that simply wouldn't be fair. But the experience has some lessons for us. The first two meals, I was fine. The next few meals, I was upset. Then I became unbearable to live with around mealtime. In time, I adjusted but just didn't like it. There came a time though where I could sit across from my wife at one of those steak houses where they bring the hot rolls and I would calmly eat my salad while she slathered more butter on all the rolls that were now hers to eat. You know, I was okay with that. I no longer had the taste for those rolls in my mouth. In fact, I could smell the yeast, and sometimes it would make me lightly nauseous. You see the first few days, I was sober of hot rolls. In time, I was clean of hot rolls.

The trap of clean and sober is this. We think because we are sober for a while that we are clean, and we let our guard down. The truth is that almost every kind of addiction works through the reward center of your brain. Your body and your mind like the pleasure feeling or the reward of feeding yourself your addiction. It becomes a roller coaster cycle. You feel pain from trauma, or you've meditated on the trauma of your past and relive the pain; you're stressed, and you don't have good coping skills; you have a self-image problem, and you're trying to stay afloat in a group that is important to you; you're lonely, depressed, angry, confused, torn, or experiencing any of the myriad of other emotional thought cycles, and so your brain says chill out and reward yourself. Sit here with me and take a load off. It'll be alright. Your problem isn't going anywhere, so enjoy yourself.

You're trying not to think these thoughts and don't know why you can't stop. It's because your brain has changed, and to a degree, you can't help yourself. Freedom from addiction, the point of being clean and being able to stay clean, is going to come only after your brain has had time to revert back to normal. Your current thinking must be subdued, and you must bring your thought life into obedience or the freedom where you rule your thought life again. Here, right here, and only in this place are you clean. The taste is out of your mouth, the feel is out of your brain, and you are back in normal reality again.

I obviously want to challenge you today to be clean and sober. The challenge is to live clean and sober in the moment, in the right now, while you also address the healing of the root of what has previously kept you in addiction. You can't win the battle of beating addiction by treating addiction as whack-a-mole arcade game. You don't break free from addiction by giving the squeaky wheel of temptation a little oil. You break free from addiction by addressing all of it in bite-size pieces one day at a time. Are you clean and sober right now? Are you addressing the trauma that produces the pain? Are you changing your environment to where addiction isn't normal and expected anymore? Are you leaning in on God your Heavenly Father to help you? Have you found a mentor to speak into your life, encourage you, and remind you of your true identity?

> **Let's pray.** Heavenly Father, I come to You again today with my friends. No matter whether they are sober or not, I am asking you to deliver them. Together we ask you to literally take the taste, the feel, and the desire for whatever addiction they have out of their mouths and out of their minds. Cleanse them from the desire and the influence, the very hold it has had on them. Cleanse their

body of the toxins that addiction has inflicted them with. Reveal to them, I pray, how to live in each moment in You and in Your strength and comfort. Speak to them and show them the way to walk in freedom. Let them experience freedom from every addiction like a breath of fresh air that lingers around us. Together, we pray that Your wisdom moves in them to align themselves with the right people in the right kind of places. Thank you, Father, for showing them how to walk in Your way that leads to life. We praise You for showing up in our lives each day.

Amen.

I'll meet you in our next conversation, "A Dead Man Did That."

A Dead Man Did That

*Therefore, **if anyone is in Christ, he is a new creation**. The old has passed away; behold, the new has come.*
2 Corinthians 5:17 (ESV)

For through the law I died to the law, so that I might live to God. I have been crucified with Christ. It is no longer I who live, but Christ who lives in me. And the life I now live in the flesh I live by faith in the Son of God, who loved me and gave himself for me.
Galatians 2:19-20 (ESV)

I want to share a very personal story with you of an old friend of mine named, well, we'll call him Tony to protect his privacy. Tony lived in a mobile home outside a very small, rural Oklahoma town. Tony was a drug dealer, user, and part-time pimp. You know, no matter how far out into the lower dark side of life, God always knows who you are and where you are at. One night, Tony was flipping the TV channels and happened to stop on a Christian TV station. Something about it drew him in first with amusement and then with his serious attention. Before he could change the channel or turn it off, Tony had prayed for God to save and deliver him.

Not many days later, Tony showed up at church on a Sunday morning looking for someplace to help him figure out how to live this "new" life he had prayed for that night. Working as an usher for that service, I met Tony and got to know him a little bit. I took an interest in Tony because that's what I do. That is what real Christians do—they care about people. It didn't take long before Tony and I were real friends. He was hungry for fellowship with people who had also been transformed by Father God. He lived in a simple yet celebratory mindset having experienced such amazing freedom. Tony pressed in hard to discover everything he could about living his new life.

In my day job, I was at that time an insurance agent. Tony wondered if he should get some life insurance, so he came over to my house one night. I explained how insurance worked, and he wanted to see if he could get some. In filling out the application, we got to the questions of have you ever used tobacco products, do you drink alcohol, have you ever used recreational drugs or abused prescription drugs, and have you ever been arrested or convicted on a drug or alcohol offense. I already knew the answer to all these questions I was asking Tony. Then, he looked at me and said he didn't know how to answer the questions. Huh? Then Tony looked at me and said, "<u>This Tony hasn't ever done any of those things. There is another Tony, who is now a dead man, who did all those things</u>. So, do I answer from the Tony I am now, or do I answer on behalf of the dead man named Tony that I was before?"

The revelation that Tony had about his new life just stunned me, and I was speechless for a few minutes. The "success" that Tony had coming out of his old lifestyle as a new Christian was far beyond anything I had witnessed in anyone else's life. Tony was dead to sin, dead to missing the mark of walking as the image of his Heavenly Father, so all Tony knew was to walk in a way to discover who he was now. He was simply walking out a life to be like his Father, his Heavenly Father who had created him, lifted him, and purposed him.

Today, maybe the most important section of this book in which we are conversing is in this question—what is your identity? Are you an addict? Are you a user? Are you weak and unable to stand against addiction? Or do you recognize that addiction has no real power, that your Heavenly Father is the eternal life that is within you, that you can live dead to the power and the pull of addiction? Dead things have no power. If you wake up in the morning and give addiction power, it will rule over you and make you serve that addiction. If you wake up in the morning and set your mind on things above, the things of God's nature in you and not on things below or the things of the lower nature, then you will experience and live the life of the Father that He created you to experience.

My challenge to you right now is repent. That means to change your mind. Change your mind to believe you have the power of God in you to live free from any and all addictions and self-defeating behaviors. Change your mind to believe that addiction has no power over you and that you are dead to all its ways and all its pulls on your mind and your body. Today is the day that you cross that threshold of no return. Father God is having an experience with you today that you can mark on the calendar and say, "Addiction died, and I am beginning to walk in and experience all the life that Father God has for me. I live only as He leads me."

Let's pray. Heavenly Father, it is a joy to come to You today, knowing that we are not stuck for eternity in our old lives. What a joy to know that "in You" we have new life and are dead to our old man. I pray today, Father, that my friends will have a revelation that a dead man has no pull, no effect, on their new lives. We thank you, Father, that Your mercies are new every morning, that You never hold our past against us, and that You are always in the now of our lives. So today, Heavenly Father, we purpose to live in the now of our lives with You. We just want to praise You for this day and this new life.

Amen.

I'll meet you in our next conversation, "Nuclear Fallout All Around."

Nuclear Fallout All Around

And after you have suffered a little while, the God of all grace, who has called you to his eternal glory in Christ, will himself restore, confirm, strengthen, and establish you. 1 Peter 5:10 (ESV)

May the God of hope fill you with all joy and peace in believing, so that by the power of the Holy Spirit you may abound in hope. Romans 15:13 (ESV)

When a nuclear bomb goes off, there is devastating destruction at the bomb site. That's not the limit of the problem, though; it's just the beginning. It's the residual nuclear fallout, the radioactive dust and explosion particles that mushroom up and are dispersed in the atmospheric winds. Those particles contaminate all the surface water and food sources up to several hundred miles away. The human body may be vaporized at the blast site, while life-threatening effects in people farther away may not show for months.

You are undoubtedly asking why we are talking about nuclear bombs and fallout while dealing with a variety of addiction issues, so let me explain. The life of an addict can look like he or she is a nuclear bomb site. Every part of an addict's being can be affected and look like scorched earth. For some addicts, it's the extreme unhealthy weight loss, the beginning of organ failure, or the mind not being able to function properly to remember, solve problems, or maintain emotional stability. Relationships get burned up, and support systems disappear to the point of having to survive and suffer on the street in homelessness.

Well, maybe you won't get to that point of loss, where everything seems like scorched earth. Life in the nuclear fallout zone loses all its swankiness too. Addiction never just affects you as the addict. The fallout of addiction travels quite deep through the family and social network of every addict. Every spouse and child suffers loss as an addict spends time, money, and health on addiction instead of investing it in family. And it's not just immediate family, like when money gets borrowed from extended family and friends and isn't repaid, or worse yet, when it gets stolen to support the addiction directly or indirectly. What about the loss to an employer who once had a good employee who started calling in sick too many times before being terminated for poor quality work and a bad attitude?

The question I need to ask you point blank is this. What has addiction cost you? And what has addiction cost those around you? Your world around you was forced to invest in your addiction because you shared that world together. In order to come out of addiction, re-enter a regular life, and see what restoration of your previous relationships is possible, you must take responsibility for the scorched earth and nuclear fallout damage that you in your addiction caused firsthand.

It is painful, but you must stop and count the cost that addiction has taken not just in your life but in the lives around you. You have not only burnt bridges, but you have accumulated a heavy debt, not just financially but in what you owe people around you in lost peace and tranquility, frayed emotions, etc.

After a nuclear bomb or reactor blows, there is the immediate emergency response to see who and what has survived and what is dead and lost. If it is a nuclear reactor that has blown up, then there is the all hands-on deck to shut it down and stop any further damage from happening. After that, it's cleanup time. It's not as simple as the intercom speaker calling out "Cleanup on aisle seven." This is a cleanup of your life and all the lives that are intertwined with your life, all the lives that were affected up close and far away.

The emergency response begins immediately, but the cleanup and effects carry on for a very long time. **I am praying right now that you comprehend** that just getting to the place of clean and sober and even understanding that you are living a new you does not mean that it is all over or that it is even easy from here on out.

As strange as this may sound, restoration and re-integrating back into a normal life will be every bit as hard as getting delivered from addiction. It will take the same personal dedication and power of God to help you walk it through to see the results. What I want to assure you of today, right here and right now, is that the joy of seeing your healing back to a whole person who is actively at work to heal the wounds that you yourself have caused is one of the greatest joys anyone can experience. The high of the mountain climber looking out from the top over everything below is only achieved by the pain of the climb.

Today, you must decide. Rather than live in the pain of addiction, will you submit to the pain of the climb back to the top of life? Can you see yourself above all the nuclear fallout of the past, looking into the beauty of a future lived in God-given freedom and restoration?

Let's pray. Heavenly Father, I come to You with my friends today with everything open before You. We know that You know our past, our present, and our future. There is nothing hidden from You. So, in humility, we bring the devastation that represents my friends' lives and circumstances before You and simply say they need restoration and healing. My friends need healing, their families need healing, and all the extended social circles that have been touched in any way by my friends' addiction need healing and restoration. We thank you today that by Your grace and mercy, You are bringing peace into all that is around us. May peace and healing flow through my friends in body, mind, soul, emotions, and in spirit. I pray the wisdom and favor of God be released in my friends and that healing and restoration be released into all the nuclear fallout caused by their past addiction. We praise You because You are the God of life and You bring us out of every area of death and defeat in our lives.

Amen.

I'll meet you in our next conversation, "Reclaiming Lost Trust."

Reclaiming Lost Trust

I give thanks to my God always for you because of the grace of God that was given you in Christ Jesus, that in every way you were enriched in him in all speech and all knowledge even as the testimony about Christ was confirmed among you so that you are not lacking in any gift, as you wait for the revealing of our Lord Jesus Christ, who will sustain you to the end, guiltless in the day of our Lord Jesus Christ. **God is faithful**, *by whom you were called into the fellowship of his Son, Jesus Christ our Lord.*
1 Corinthians 1:4-9 (ESV)

Trust isn't really something you lose. It's not like forgetting where you put down the car keys and if you look long enough, you'll find the lost trust. No, trust is something you earn through honesty, integrity, faithfulness, and openness. It is much like your reputation in that it takes a long time to develop and a short time to ruin. When I deal with people in the area of trust, they often bemoan, "Why won't people trust me?" or "Why won't so-and-so trust me?" In their minds, they are being honest or at least have every good intention at that moment. So, what's the problem? I'm glad you asked. I've made a list of ways that people ruin trust so that it becomes a serious relationship issue.

Number one is a trail behind you of broken promises like, "I won't use anymore," or "I promise I won't spend the grocery money on the stuff." Next would be lying and manipulating the feelings and decision-making of those who are closest to you or trying to help you. The biggest of these is guilting people into doing something for you. Or how about demanding or manipulating people into doing something for you and then not being there for them? And lastly, how about downright deceitfulness, like telling your family how they should be proud of you because you are clean and sober while you put on your jacket to go snort the powder you bought after leaving the pawn shop?

The truth is that trust is earned, and trust is easily burnt. The place and the way to reclaim lost trust is to begin by being honest with yourself. You are the person you have lied to the most. Every time you said, "I don't have a problem with addiction," or "I can quit anytime," you knew that was a lie. Every time you said, "This is the last time I'm going to steal something and turn it into cash or drugs," and you already had your next conniving thievery planned out, you were lying to yourself and burning your own trust.

Let me just say it this way. The most important person for you to earn trust from is always yourself. The truth is, once you have been in addiction and scorched the earth around your life, no one is going to trust you until you behave in a way that you can trust yourself. Not until you trust yourself when no one is looking is anyone going to trust you, even when he or she is watching you. So, rebuilding trust starts with you being honest to yourself.

There are some other keys to rebuilding trust that I want to share with you. When people are trying to learn to trust you again, they will look at your eyes, listen to the tone of your voice, watch your body language, and judge your attitude for marks of humility and patience. Re-earning trust is as big as a final exam over the whole last years of your life.

How about some things that reclaiming lost trust is not about? It's not about people continuing to give you handouts, loans, or any other financial access. Maybe you conned people into using their credit card or, even worse, stole it for fraudulent purposes. They don't have to give you their credit card again to prove they trust you again. That smells of another con game. If you need help and if they decide to help again, then the way to start reclaiming trust is to present ALL the information around your need and be open to answering questions and letting them verify your answers. If you are worthy of being trusted any little bit, then you will be patient, open, and understanding. And if they hear you out and decline to help in this situation, then you will respect their decision and politely excuse yourself to find another solution. As an adult, no one owes you anything. And as people whose trust you previously lost, it's all on you to show one action and interaction at a time over potentially a long period of time that you can be trusted again.

The principle you must remember is this. People will not trust you with big things until they can trust you repeatedly with the little things. It's about consistently doing right until others notice (even if they don't when you think they should). Everything matters—every situation, every action, every reaction, every day, and every night. People all around you are going to be watching to see if your new life is a mirage or if you are real and if you are stable.

Here is my challenge to you today—take a long look in the mirror. Tell yourself what you see. Tell yourself how you feel about yourself. Answer this question in the mirror for loved ones of yours—are their lives, their reputations, their finances, and their peace of mind safe in your hands and in your actions? Are you humble enough to offer a sincere apology for any and all hurt or loss you may have caused, and have you offered to make retribution as you can?

Lastly, you need to understand the need for you to have patience with others as you seek to reclaim lost trust. Those around you may have Post Trust Stress Disorder, and even the thought of trusting you again may trigger a PTSD response. To have lost their trust means you have hurt them, and you must give them time to heal again. In the meantime, <u>the most important person for you to work on regaining trust with again is always going to be you</u>.

Let's pray. Heavenly Father, my friends and I come to You today consumed with the thought that You are faithful and that You are trustworthy. We know that You live and move and have Your being in each of us. Together, we are coming to the understanding that faithfulness lives in us and trustworthiness lives in us by Your Spirit. So today, we ask You to help us to walk each day in a greater understanding that we are faithful and trustworthy. I just speak to my friends today that they are trustworthy—that they walk consistently as a new person in Christ, free from addiction and free from all the past broken promises and con games. I thank you for self-trust and honesty within my friends that becomes so consistent that their peers and those watching them cannot help but take notice. We praise You that You have repaired the broken moral compass of my friends for all to see.

Amen.

I'll meet you in our next conversation, "Re-entering Regular Life."

Re-entering Regular Life

Humble yourselves, therefore, under the mighty hand of God so that at the proper time he may exalt you, casting all your anxieties on him, because he cares for you.
1 Peter 5:6-7 (ESV)

You know, I debated whether to talk with you about reclaiming lost trust or re-entering regular life first. Obviously, reclaiming lost trust won, but you could say regaining trust is the first step to re-entering regular life. In a way, I have discussed much of this subject in the previous chapters. For instance, to re-enter regular life, you will have to pass by the wide-open traps without getting caught this go round. You will need a mentor, someone who you have given permission to speak into your life with full honesty to help review your progress and warn you of the pitfalls. You are going to need a support system that is larger than one individual, meaning people who know you in the different areas of your life. People who speak to you about integrity, finances, attitudes, spiritual development, character traits in action, dealing with social pressure, goal setting, work ethic, and dealing with rejection and setbacks. You are going to need life coaches to help you be a winning team again.

There are some things I want to say to you right now though without you having to wait to hear them from one of your future mentors or coaches. Remember that addiction didn't destroy your life and scorch your circumstances in a single day. And restoring and re-entering a regular or normal life will take time also. To accomplish it, you will have to commit to the long haul. There are no shortcuts to rebuilding a strong foundation. If you take shortcuts, you will fall again, and it will be harder and take longer to stand back up again.

You must redeem your time. You've probably wasted years and maybe even the prime of your life. You don't have any time to waste. Every day is precious. Every relationship is precious. Every resource in your hand or that comes into your hand is precious. Treat it all with value and the respect it deserves. If you manage your day and your days right, your best years can be your future. Believe it. Live it. Every day.

To most of the people around you, you will represent what you became in the downhill slide toward self-destruction. To them, it's about what you did and how you failed. This simply cannot be how you think about yourself or how you see yourself. To you, **it's always about showing who you are now**. It's about demonstrating the real you that your Heavenly Father made and not letting any previous behavior define you in your own eyes. You need to understand that you can't make others change their minds about you, but you can live your changed mind about you until they change theirs. That's all you can do, and that's what you must do every day for as long as it takes.

Here is the bottom-line principle. Going forward, you are going to live your life not to please men when they watch you but as if you are only living your life to please your Heavenly Father, who sees you in public and even in secret. <u>If you please Him, He will exalt you in the eyes of others in due time</u>. Trust Him!

I want to leave you with this illustration. A man is driving through the countryside on a beautiful sunshiny day. He comes across this sagging barn out in the field with a rusted old '57 Chevy out front. He whips his car around to drive up the old farmer's driveway to offer to buy the piece of rusted junk metal and get it out of the farmer's field. He comes back with a flatbed and carefully winches up the remains onto the truck. He takes it home, cleans out his garage, and sets it down. Years go by before he opens the door and drives out the beautifully restored car. The rusted junker that barely made it home for a $100 is now worth over $25,000. The junker that thousands passed by and never wanted nor had interest in is now wanted by everyone. The man took the unwanted junker home and spent time in private healing it and restoring it far beyond the original value.

This could be the story of your life. Do you see a collector's item in the junk of your old life? Are you willing to spend the time in private to heal and to let others work on and speak into your life? Will you submit to the process of being restored over time into right thought patterns, healing one old relationship at a time, starting one new habit, and letting your Heavenly Father restore and polish you so you can be sent out as a vessel of honor, far more than people first saw in you?

> **Let's pray.** Heavenly Father, as we come to You today, we are at another critical time in my friends' lives. We want to thank you for every victory, both big and small, in coming out of addiction. I want to thank you especially for Your patience with my friends as they have come out of darkness into the light of life. I am thankful that You have loved them all along their journey. Father, we are actively looking for Your wisdom and Your favor as my friends begin to acclimate back into a regular, normal life without addiction. We praise You that You continue to work in my friends' lives as they move into the rebuilding phase. We thank you in advance for every new door You open of healthy relationships,

employment opportunities, and the restoration of houses and cars needed to do life. We praise You that You bring people, places, and things together for my friends to bring them into their destinies.

Amen.

I'll meet you in our next conversation, "Living with Passion and Purpose."

Living with Passion and Purpose

I know what I'm doing. I have it all planned out—plans to take care of you, not abandon you, plans to give you the future you hope for.
Jeremiah 29:11 (MSG)

By now, you are fully aware that addiction is very "me"- centered. When you were an addict, everything revolved around your addiction, your mood swings, your spending to support it, your quest to find it, your lost days living in a daze when those around you needed you and everyone caught up in a constant worry and anxiety over you.

The thing about living "from" a God-given purpose is this—God is love (1 John 4:8). The God kind of love is extroverted by nature. The God kind of love flows out of us to love our neighbor. Love is "other"-centered as it flows out from within us. Because you are made in the image of God, when you live your God-given purpose, His image moves "you" out from the center of your life and moves Him into the center.

If you were to tell me that you don't know your God-given purpose, it would not surprise me. That seems to be common among people I visit with on this subject. I think that is because we either think God isn't involved in our lives at that level or on the complete flipside of that thinking, it's overwhelming to think of God involved in the complexity of our whole lives. So, let me see if I can help simplify it for you.

Your first and foremost purpose in life is the same as it was the first man God created. His name was Adam. God made Adam in His image. So, your purpose is to be like Him. Wow! I know that's a bombshell. Here we have spent time getting free from the god of addiction, getting healed to get back into regular life, and now we've got to be like God?

Okay, relax. Let me explain how it's not as mind-blowing a thought as you first may think. The Bible says you are the temple or the dwelling place of God. His Spirit lives in you, so His life is your real life. If God lives in you by His Spirit, then His nature and character are already in you. Your most important job now is to live His life out through your body instead of the low life of selfish addiction that you once lived. It is now less of you and more of Him.

Hopefully, you understand that your doing flows out of your being. So, if your being is God in you, then your doing is His character that is in you. That means the fruit of the Spirit, which is love, joy, peace, patience, kindness, goodness, faithfulness, gentleness, and self-control (Galatians 5:22-23), is the fruit of your life. The purpose of God is for you to show the world around you His nature and character within you expressed outwardly as the fruit or actions of the Spirit of God toward others.

Another purpose that is so important to grasp is God the Father's desire for you to be planted in a family and not to be isolated and separated from others. Psalm 68:6 (ESV) says, "God settles the solitary in a home; he leads out the prisoners to prosperity, but the rebellious dwell in a parched land." While past addiction has probably cost you family and friends, God wants to replant you in relationships that will be as family to you—relationships that are safe and will believe in you, encourage you, teach you, and admonish or correct you in love. There will be a church family where you can grow in Christ, practice walking your new life, and be equipped for the ministry that the Father has for you.

There is so much about purpose I would like to share with you. But **the last thing I want to share with you for now** is this—3 John 1:2 (ESV) says, "Beloved, I pray that all may go well with you and that you may be in good health, as it goes well with your soul." God your Father purposes that things go well with you, that you live as He has planned for you, that you be in health, that your whole being prospers. That's not about "get rich quick" and everything being easy. That's about living His nature and character, living in healthy relationships, and living in total-man health. It's about living a transformed life and transforming lives around you because of what God the Father has done in you.

Now, let's talk a little bit about passion before we move on. When we move off the self-centered throne of our life, we discover there is a driving passion within us that must be expressed. It's what gets us up in the morning living with joy, zest, and vitality. Your passion will be something that you will have to do. You may work at XYZ company building widgets by day, but the paycheck from XYZ company will be the source of income so you can do your passion otherwise. For instance, Donna and I own a restaurant. <u>Our passion is healing hurting people</u>. We cook food and deliver it to tables of people who end up telling us the woes of their lives. We make meals and go out on the streets and feed hungry people, looking for the opportunity to visit and pray with them. <u>The restaurant is a tool to connect us with people</u>.

Your passion will be connected to something that riles you up, which is probably an injustice that you need to help make right or a need you see that is not being filled in people's lives. There is a people group that God has called you to minister to, and that people group will reveal the passion within you that keeps life from being mundane and boring. <u>The greatest high in life is to make a difference in the world around you</u>.

Let's pray. Heavenly Father, this is an awesome day. It is a day that You have made to enjoy us and to walk with us. It is a little overwhelming to think that we can descend into the darkness of addiction and that You can bring us up and out into the light of life and still have purpose for our lives. We thank you that my friends are even now feeling a new passion just to live in the freedom of relationship with You. We pray specifically right now that my friends will discover the joy and passion of living Your life as them each day—the passion to be Your expression of Your nature and character and especially of Your love, grace, and mercy to others. We praise You for revealing Your plans, purposes, and passions in the everyday of a restored life. Thank you for never leaving nor forsaking us or our purpose. We commit ourselves to You from this day forward.

Amen.

I'll meet you in our next conversation, "Telling Your Story."

Telling Your Story

But in your hearts honor Christ the Lord as holy, always being prepared to make a defense to anyone who asks you for a reason for the hope that is in you; yet do it with gentleness and respect. 1 Peter 3:15 (ESV)

A most amazing incident happened to me a few days ago. I was going over the draft text of these conversations for this book with a man that my wife and I took off the streets of OKC into our home a few years ago. I was soliciting his feedback on how this book was coming together. As we were finishing up, a customer came over and apologized for the interruption, proceeding to tell us he couldn't help but overhear our conversation. He wanted to tell us that he was 2 years, 5 months, and 19 days clean. Needless to say, we celebrated with him. I think he was telling me that I was on the right track to help people have success like he was experiencing.

There does come a time to tell your story. Testimonies, though, can be a minefield. How many times have you heard someone tell a whopper fish story like, "My doctor says I had the worst case of xyz he had ever seen?" Listen, it is so important for people to hear that someone overcame addiction and be challenged that they too can overcome addiction. But **don't embellish your testimony**. Don't try to star in the soap opera, *As the Addiction Turns*. Remember, pride goes before a fall. You don't want to have the biggest recovery only to follow it with the biggest fall. Simply celebrate and encourage others with what has really happened. Your honesty and sincerity in telling your story is what will make it powerful and real to someone else.

There is a biblical saying of, "Don't cast your pearls before swine (Matthew 7:6)." This means to reserve yourself to speak only to those who will receive and honor your message. Use some wisdom to determine which audience you speak to about your journey. Sometimes the drama queens of those you were in addiction with can't wait to razz you, belittle you, and reject your newfound clean as hypocritical and prophesy your impending relapse. But sometimes, when the ones who were in addiction with you see you come out, it is just what they needed to give them hope that they too can be free. My advice is to just be transparent, humbly share the progress you have made, be honest about what you still struggle with, and encourage others to ask their Heavenly Father to help them break free. Share what a mentor has done for you in accountability and how being honest that you had an addiction and needed help was the beginning of your breaking free.

Whatever you do, don't talk down or belittle others who have not started or made it as far as you have in your journey to freedom. Express empathy, but always speak to their potential to be and to live free from addiction. Your story could be the glimmer of hope that shines for someone else to follow you in a journey to freedom and transformation. And as much as anything, hearing your own story out of your mouth with your own ears encourages you. Your testimony glorifies your Heavenly Father, who sent Jesus the Christ to show us we could live free from every bondage, even the one you battled until you found victory.

Now it's time to live whole again and to take the power of God to live whole again to the streets. Remember, healed people no longer hurt people; they are totally invested in healing others.

Let's pray. Heavenly Father, we celebrate today the awesomeness of the journey that You led my friends through from addiction to freedom, from pain to joy, and from loss to blessing. You are the God of divine appointment, and we know that my friends futures are filled with divine appointments to tell their story. Whether it be one-to-one or one-to-many, I pray my friends remain humble, knowing that it is You who gives us the victory as You work to bring life to all our being. I thank you that in every situation, wisdom, humility, and compassion flow out of my friends to whoever they find to minister to. We praise You that my friends' stories are not over but just getting to the best part, the part of being used by You to heal and encourage others.

Amen.

I'll meet you on the streets to learn your name and listen to your story. I can't wait to see you clean and sober, living your God-given purpose and passion, and watch you tell others your story of how an experience with your Heavenly Father saved, transformed, and restored your life.

We love you.

Pastor Wayne and Donna
Grace United Urban Ministry
GUUM.faith

"Taking the Power to Live Whole Again to the Streets"

Lightning Source UK Ltd.
Milton Keynes UK
UKHW021851200520
363522UK00010B/223